Angels Anonymous
God's Undercover Angels

By
Jo-Ellen Goodall

PublishAmerica
Baltimore

ISBN: 1-4241-1317-2
PUBLISHED BY
PUBLISHAMERICA, LLLP.
www.publishamerica.com
Baltimore

Printed in the United States of America

To all of my Undercover Angels…you know who you are!
Thanks a million!

Chapters

Chapter 1
The Invasion

THERE ARE WARS GOING ON, BATTLES between good and evil. Although most of us might not see the wars, they are raging around us every day. Many people do not realize what is at stake. The wars are not for our homes or property, but for our very souls. It is not one single war, but a war for every single person on earth. In other words, you have your war and I have mine. Each one is different, with varying tactics from both sides. But who is fighting these wars?

We are battling evil every day and God has sent his troops to earth to help us in our battles. They are not bloody fights, but subtle spiritual struggles and the battlefields are our everyday lives. Our guardian angels stand beside us, they are sent by God to protect us from the evil that surrounds us day after day. The choices that we make influence the way that our war is going. If we choose to follow God then we are empowering our guardian angels to fight away the evil, but if we choose to follow the evil ways we give that power away. The choice is ours and we must choose wisely because our very souls depend on it!

> "Put on the full armor of God so that you can take a stand against the devil's schemes. For our struggle is not against flesh and blood, but against the rulers, against the authorities, against the powers of this dark world and against the spiritual forces of evil in the heavenly realms" (Ephesians 6:11-12).

The Father loves us so very much and wants us all to be with Him in His Heavenly Kingdom. Satan wants us, not because he loves us, but because he doesn't want us to be with God. He will do whatever it takes to ensure that we never reach Heaven. Evil takes many forms and is not afraid to walk among us because it hides behind the mask of goodness. If we saw evil in its true hideous form, we would run to our Heavenly Father and hold on to Him forever, but evil is well disguised and tricks us with its beautiful façade and "live it up" attitude.

So the Father has sent another Army, one that is also in disguise. He knows that if we see them as they truly are we would flock to them and seek their protection, but God wants us to freely choose the path of goodness. This army does not carry conventional weapons, but is armed only with a sword of love… a love that is pure and unconditional. Because God is Love and love is good and pure, it will conquer evil. We just have to have Faith!

So just what is this new army that God has sent? Where are they hiding? They walk among us every day and touch every aspect of our lives. Their influence is changing us little by little. Some were sent here on a mission, others were recruited to help spread their work. But just who are they and what do they want?

They are the Undercover Angels, God's earthly army, agents sent by Him to help us in our daily life. It is not an elite group but one that is made up of ordinary people who do extraordinary things. No, they don't walk among us with their wings spread or their halos shining for all to see, they don't hide in the shadows and they aren't invisible. The Undercover Angels blend into our society. They work and play side by side with us every day. Some of the Undercover Angels are not of our world, but that of our Father's Heavenly Kingdom. The rest were recruited, some unknowingly, to be an Undercover Angel. Slowly, their presence is being felt and their influence is spreading.

When we say that the Undercover Angels are everywhere we turn—they are actually everywhere—in our schools, malls, businesses, small towns, and large cities. They could be our family members, friends, co-workers, or total strangers. We never know who might be a member of the Undercover Angels. It is a secret guild that has an unparalleled impact on us all.

We bump into them in the hallways of our schools. They hand us our packages at the checkout counter, deliver our mail, or take care of our car insurance. They could be a doctor, policeman, fireman, secretary, or even a telemarketer. It doesn't matter who they are or what they do, the only requirement to be an Undercover Angels is to follow the Lord's Will and help to spread His Message. All are welcome to join, no one who is truly willing to serve the Lord and His mission is turned away. The Undercover Angels are here to help us live better and to follow the path of goodness. Their mission is from God to give comfort, advice, and help to us when we need it the most.

Have you ever had a bad day and just when you feel you can't take it any longer someone comes along and gives you a "pick-me-up" compliment, a hug, or even a smile? That person could be a member of the Undercover Angels. They are the ones who make us smile, who makes us feel like we are important—that our existence counts. They give advice to us to help us make the right decision. Sometimes we listen and sometimes we don't, but no matter what choices we make, they are still standing beside us ready to help us again. To them no one is a lost cause. Everyone is valuable…every life has worth and a purpose. They are here to help us fulfill that purpose, which is to love one another, and to honor, and serve our Heavenly Father.

Chapter 2
The Pretenders and Users

WE MUST BE CAUTIOUS BECAUSE THERE are those who pretend to be members of the Undercover Angels, but their purpose is one of deception. They deceive us with their lies of helping others. They are not interested in our spiritual or even physical well-being but only their own self-centered interests... they are takers...givers of grief and strife. If we follow these people, they will lead us to our eternal demise.

So how do we know when we have met a pretender? We must take a step back from the situation if we can and ask ourselves— "What will they gain from my decision?" If their only gain is to see you benefit from their help then they are truly Undercover Angels. However, if they only want to help you so that they can say, "Look, what I have done!" then they are not Undercover Angels, but pretenders.

There are many examples of the pretenders. One illustration would be people who extend help to a runaway by providing food and shelter and then introduce that young boy or girl to a life of drugs, alcohol, and prostitution. What had started out to be a "lifesaver" actually turned out to be a "life-taker." These people were only interested in their own selfish desires not that of the young runaway's who was looking for help—for someone to care about them.

Then there are the "good neighbors" or "friends" who come to help you during a troubled time in your life. Their help is appreciated and you believe that they really cared about what you went through, but then you discovered that they were there only to gather all the "juicy" details so that they could tell others about your problems. These people wear the disguise of an Undercover Angel, but are just another example of a pretender. They use you to get what they want and then move on to another unsuspecting victim.

"In fact, everyone who wants to live a godly life in Christ Jesus will be persecuted, while evil men and imposters will go from bad to worse, deceiving and being deceived" (2 Timothy 3:13).

There are many who accept help from the Undercover Angels but think only of themselves and do not repay the good deeds by helping others or spreading God's message. These people are "users." They show no gratitude for the help they received. They take what they can get and run. We may even see these people in the pews of our churches every Sunday. Good intentions pave the way to Hell unless they are done with the true intention of helping others. Those deeds done for any other purpose are not that of the Father's will, but that of Satan.

The way to the Father is not easy, but with the help of our guardian angels and the Undercover Angels we can overcome all the obstacles, which are laid before us by Satan and his minions. With the help of the Angels, who clear our path, our walk with the Father gets easier and easier. It is said that it is easy to be bad...but it is hard to be good. The Undercover Angels along with our guardian angels will help us walk that path of goodness, if we choose to let them.

Sometimes we seek help in the wrong places. We look at the places that give us instant gratification or instant help, but we fail to look where we should. We need to turn to the Lord for help in all things big or small and ask for His forgiveness for our sins. However to be forgiven, we must first forgive those who have sinned against us and give all things in our life over to God. When we do this, our burdens are lifted and our way is made clear. This is the message that the Undercover Angels were sent to deliver. We don't need to look for them, they will find us. It might be today, tomorrow, or a month from now, but they will find us. Will we recognize them and accept their help or will we turn our backs and go our own way?

Once an Undercover Angel has touched our life the only payment that is asked of us is to repay their act of kindness by helping others who are in need. The phrase *"One good deed deserves another"* is true. If we all practiced that phrase then there would be a ripple effect that would take place. Everyone would be helping their neighbors instead of fighting with them. So, when we freely help others, without the "what's in it for me?" attitude, we are volunteering to become members of God's earthly army, the Undercover Angels.

The following stories are actual accounts
of Undercover Angels in our everyday lives.

Chapter 3
The Reunion

SOMETIMES UNDERCOVER ANGELS APPEAR IN THE strangest places. This is a story of Della, an elderly widow with a smile of gold and a voice like heaven. Della received a call one afternoon from a niece, Mary Jo, which she hadn't seen or heard from in 37 years. Mary Jo was only a year old when her aunt last saw her. After her parents divorced, Mary Jo never saw her father or his family again. Now, as a fast approaching middle-aged woman, she was working on her family's genealogy and called her aunt to try to get some information on her father's family history.

Mary Jo nervously made that phone call to Della after getting the number from an operator. When Della answered the phone, Mary Jo reintroduced herself to her aunt and told her that she was interested in the family history. What came from her aunt's lips were words Mary Jo had longed to hear, "We think about you often and we love you." As tears began to well up in Mary Jo's eyes her only reply was, "Really?" Della reassured her that the family had not forgotten her in all the lost years.

They talked about their families and how Mary Jo had twin sons who were at a camp not far from where Della lived and that she would be picking them up from there the next day. Della then asked if she and the boys could stop and see her. When Mary Jo agreed to stop and see her aunt what happened next was totally unexpected. "Your father will be here too, he is in town for a reunion. He would love to see you again and meet the boys," Della said. Now Mary Jo hadn't seen her father since she was a year old, so she had no memories of him. For fear of rejection, she tried to back out of the visit, but her aunt persisted that she stop by and get reacquainted with her family. "Your father is a wonderful man and I know that he would love to see you again," her aunt said.

Early that next morning, Mary Jo, anxious and nervous about the potential meeting, drove first to the camp and picked up her sons and then to her Aunt Della's to finally meet her family. After a short visit with her Aunt Della, Mary Jo's father walked in the back door. He had no idea that she and her sons were there. When Della introduced Mary Jo and the boys to him he began to cry and gave them all a hug. Then he looked at his daughter and said, "I have thought of you every day...God I love you!" Mary Jo never realized it, but that was something that she longed for and needed to hear.

As they visited, they found out that they only lived a short distance away from each other. So they agreed to have another visit so that Mary Jo could meet the rest of the family.

Della, as an Undercover Angel, brought these two individuals together and helped to heal a family. Although the lost years between a father and his daughter cannot be replaced they can now start the process of healing and building a new relationship.

Della was sent as an Undercover Angel to help bring this family together. Mary Jo could have easily turned down her aunt's invitation to meet, but there was something in Della's voice that persuaded Mary Jo to come to her house and meet her father. It was God's plan and Della was the instrument, which He used to facilitate His propose.

"'You are my witness,' declares the Lord, 'and my servant whom I have chosen'" (Isaiah 43:10).

Chapter 4
Lending a Hand

STEVE WAS A HIGH SCHOOL TEACHER. He worked with the students and helped them to achieve their educational goals. But he had a secret life, one that even his wife of 12 years did not know about. She only discovered his secret right before his death.

Steve was diagnosed with ALS, also known as Lou Gehrig's disease, and was eventually unable to work. The degenerative muscle disease took its toll on the family physically, emotionally, and financially. Soon word spread around the community that Steve was gravely ill.

The amount of people who came to help him and his family during this time was beyond belief. Apparently, Steve had not only helped his students learn their chemistry, but he also helped those students whose family could not afford to buy groceries and clothing. Every pay Steve would buy needed items for the disadvantaged families of the students in his school. He never told anyone that he was doing this…it was between him and God.

He had touched the lives of so many people and made such a difference in the students' lives that they did what they could to help him. They held benefit concerts, basketball games, and dinners to help his family defray the cost of medical bills. Through those events, his wife discovered that he had been using the money from his second job to help his students and their families make ends meet.

Steve, a devout Catholic, was living his faith. He helped others who were less fortunate and he was making a difference. When his wife asked why he never told her what he had done for these people, Steve said he wasn't doing it for the glory, but just to give back the Blessings that he had been given.

Although he passed away at the age of 41, his influence continues to be felt to this day by many people. He made a lasting impact on all of those that he came into contact with. Steve was a true Undercover Angel. His unselfish acts were truly from the heart. He lived God's message and helped to spread His Word.

"Carry each other's burdens, and in this way you will fulfill the laws of Christ" (Galatians 6:2).

Chapter 5
Cyber Angel

AGAIN, UNDERCOVER ANGELS CAN APPEAR AT anytime and at any place. This story is about Gene, who during the day is a truck driver, but at night he is an avid computer gamer. His online gaming introduced him to many different people and many evenings he will chat with his newfound "buddies."

Now one evening a young lady, Sally, started to chat about how she had nothing to live for and how she wanted to end it all. Assuming that it was a teenager fooling around in the chat room, no one in the chat paid attention to her cries for help, but Gene, being a born-again Christian, took the chance that this might be real and talked to her about her purpose in life and that God loved her. He persuaded Sally to call him at home.

That evening she did call him, Gene used that opportunity to spread God's message of love by witnessing to her. They talked for hours and he was able to convince Sally not to take her own life, but give her life and her problems to God. He kept telling her that God has a plan for her…that she has a purpose in this life. Gene told Sally that God loved her unconditionally and it didn't matter what she had done in the past, what matters is what she does now. Then Gene reminded her that yesterday is in the past, tomorrow has yet to arrive, but today is a gift…a gift from God and that's why it is called the present.

Sally must have heeded his words because today she is an ordained minister working as a counselor for those who have attempted suicide. What would have happened to her if Gene hadn't talked to her about God? What if she hadn't listened to him and she turned away from the Father? How many lives would have been affected if she had in fact taken her own life? We may never know the answers to those questions, but we do know that one person can affect the lives of hundreds and even thousands of people with one small gesture.

Gene made a difference in Sally's life and in return she is now influencing those whom she is counseling. Gene recruited Sally as an Undercover Angel and now she is spreading God's message. The saying *"you reap what you sow"* is certainly fitting in this story because Gene's love for his fellow man helped to save Sally and all those that she has come into contact with.

"Dear children, let us not love with words or tongue but with actions and in truth" (1 John 3:18).

Chapter 6
Staying Afloat

JOE HAD JUST GRADUATED FROM HIGH school and was vacationing at the beach with his family. He always loved to ride the waves on his boogie board, but one day was different.

It was early afternoon and the waves seemed perfect. Joe and his brother grabbed their boogie boards and headed out into the surf. As they were enjoying the thrill of the breakers, Joe noticed that an older man was not a strong swimmer and had swum out farther than what he should. At first the man appeared to be riding the waves, but then Joe noticed that the man had gone under the water a few times. He remembered from his first aid training that that was a sign of drowning. Something told Joe to act and act fast!

The man was struggling to stay afloat. No one seemed to notice that this man was in distress. Joe swam over to him. Trying to remember the steps to use when helping a person who may be drowning, Joe tried to give the man his board to help him stay afloat and he tried to talk to him to keep him calm, but that only made the man panic more. In his fright, the man fought Joe every step of the way and somehow snapped that board in two. He grabbed at Joe and tried to use him as a float. As the waves crashed against him, Joe struggled to hold the terrified man above the water. The salt water was burning Joe's eyes and he began to realize that he had to do something different.

Finally, taking a deep breath Joe dove under the man and lifted him up so that he could stay above water. The man kept kicking and thrashing about in the water. With his body now aching all over from being kicked and punched by the terrified man, Joe held the man up so that his head was above the water. Joe would come up for short breaths of air and then dive back down swimming a few feet closer to shore each time trying to get the man to safety. At last, the lifeguards saw what was happening and they came to help in the rescue.

When the lifeguards reached the scene they helped to pull the man from the ocean. They saw that the man was about six feet four inches tall and weighed approximately three hundred pounds and then they looked at Joe who weighed about one hundred and thirty-five pounds and was only about five feet ten inches tall. One lifeguard gazed at Joe and said, "Do you realize that he could have brought you down with him?" Joe's only reply was, "Yeah, but something made me go over there before I had time to think about what could have happened." The lifeguard just smiled and said that Joe probably saved this man's life.

By now a crowd had gathered around to see what was going on and the man's family came running over. The lifeguards spoke with them and then pointed to Joe who was leaving with his broken board. The man's wife came up to him and thanked him for saving her husband and said, "You're a real lifesaver, young man…today you were my husband's guardian angel." Then she hugged Joe and offered to replace his board. Joe sheepishly thanked her but said it was time for a new one anyway. As Joe

walked away he thought for a minute and just shook his head...
Me a guardian angel?

He wasn't the man's guardian angel, but was a volunteer, recruited by the Undercover Angels. That "something" that made him risk his life to aid a stranger was actually God telling him to help. Joe answered the Lord's call, but how many of us would have done what he did? How many of us look the other way because we don't want to get involved. What would have happened if Joe ignored the whole situation and thought that the lifeguards would handle it because that is their job?

Today's teens are labeled as selfish and self-centered. The news only tells of those who are in trouble with the law not the good that they do. Joe's actions never made the news. What he did was put the need of another, a stranger, ahead of his own. His actions weren't unique, actually there are many teens who answer the Lord's call and are members of the Undercover Angels, but we rarely hear of their good deeds or sacrifices.

"And do not forget to do good and to share with others, for with such sacrifices God is pleased" (Hebrews 13:16).

Chapter 7
New Shoes

JOHN WAS SO EXCITED WHEN HE woke up for school. Today was the first day of basketball practice. He was going to be a member of the school's instructional team. It was a team for those boys learning the game of basketball. John was confident that he would be able to be a starter for the team because he had been practicing all summer.

He went to the gym after school and was changing his clothes in the locker room when he noticed another boy, Paul, sitting in the corner crying. John walked over to him and asked what was wrong. Paul informed him that his mother never brought his gym shoes to school and now he couldn't practice. John knew that Paul's family didn't have much money and that he probably didn't have the shoes required to be on the team.

John told Paul that his mother might still bring them and that he should talk with the coach. The little boy looked at John and, with tears streaming down his face, said, "I did and he told me that I couldn't be on the team unless I had gym shoes." John didn't know what to say. He finished getting dressed and then went to the coach and asked if he could go home for a minute. Knowing that John only lived down the street, the coach told John he could but that he would have to run a lap for every minute he was late for practice. John looked at the coach and said, "That's okay…this is really important." The coach was shocked when John said that he didn't mind running laps. He thought for sure that John still wouldn't want to run home if he knew that he would have to run laps.

John ran as fast as he could home. He burst through the front door and yelled something to his mother as he darted up the stairs. When he arrived at his room he reached under his bed and grabbed a bag and off he went. He flew down the stairs and was out the front door in a flash.

When John arrived at the gym the boys were already doing their warm-up exercises. The coach yelled over to him, "You owe me seven laps, Johnny!" John acknowledged the coach with a head nod and then dashed into the locker room. Paul was still there, too embarrassed to leave the corner. John looked at him and then threw the bag over to him. John then turned and went back out to be with the rest of the team.

When John reached the court, the coach asked him what he had to get. John said that he had to get something for someone. With that the coach told him that he was now up to nine because he took additional time going into the locker room. The coach yelled at him, "Just because you won the State Foul Shooting Contest last week, don't think you can do just whatever you want! You will be at practice on time every day just like the rest of the team!"

Paul opened the bag and inside was a new pair of gym shoes. He remembered how John told the boys in the class that he had saved up all of his allowance to buy a special pair of gym shoes for the upcoming basketball season. Paul couldn't believe that

John was giving him the shoes he had saved up for. He quickly put them on…they fit perfectly. He finished dressing and went to join the others at practice.

When Paul walked on the court the coach gave a stern look and barked directions at him. Paul joined in the practice with the other boys. The time seemed to go fast and soon the coach called all the boys together for a team meeting. When practice broke the coach yelled to Johnny to start his nine laps.

As John began running his laps Paul went to the other boys and asked why John had to run. He was told that John was late for practice and the coach was angry with him because he ran home to get something. Then Paul looked at his feet and went to the coach to explain why John was late. Paul approached the coach and told him that John was late because he ran home to get him a pair of gym shoes so that he could practice with the team. He said, "Coach, please don't make him run anymore. He got into trouble because of me." With that the coach looked away from Paul and stared at John. He thought for a minute about what he had said to him at practice. He told Paul to go and catch his ride home.

Now the coach started to feel a little embarrassed and called for John. John ran over to him and said, "I'm not done, Coach…I still have three laps to go." The coach asked him why he didn't tell him that he went home to get shoes for Paul. John replied that he didn't want anyone to know what he did and that it was no big deal. But the coach disagreed. "It is a big deal! Johnny, you cared enough about him to risk my wrath! Weren't those the shoes you just bought?" John nodded his head yes.

Paul ran over to John and thanked him for his shoes. Then he ran to his mother and told her what John had done. She looked at John in disbelief, and then she and Paul turned and left the gym. The coach looked at John and told him he didn't have to run anymore and that he needed to go get changed. As John walked into the locker room, his brother, who was also on the team, said,

"What are you going to tell Mom about your shoes?" John said that he wasn't going to tell his mother anything. But that would change.

When the boys returned home from practice, their mother was on the phone. She looked particularly at John and motioned for him to sit on the couch. When she hung up the phone she told John that his basketball coach had just called and informed her about what John had done that day. John was sure she would be mad because those shoes cost so much money. She asked John why he gave the shoes away and he answered, "God teaches us to help the poor and to Love our neighbors as ourselves, so I was just doing what God wanted." His mother couldn't argue with that she just smiled and said how proud she was of him.

Although it was only a pair of shoes, John showed that compassion has no age limit. He knew that he should help Paul because that is what God wanted him to do. John volunteered to be a part of God's Earthly Army. As a member of the Undercover Angels, he touched and changed many lives that day. John showed Paul, his coach, the team, and his own mother just how much he cared for others. What an unselfish act to give away something that one has saved up for so that someone else may benefit from it! How many of us would have given away a new pair of shoes or accepted a punishment when we knew that what we did was to help someone? John surely understands, lives, and believes the phrase *"Do unto others as you would have done to you."*

"In everything I did, I showed you that by this kind of hard work we must help the weak, remembering the words of the Lord Jesus himself said: 'It is more blessed to give than to receive'" (Acts 20:35).

Chapter 8
The Great Flood

IT WAS A RAINY SEPTEMBER DAY in the foothills of West Virginia. The remnants of Hurricane Ivan were making its presence known. Just over a week ago, the area had already had received three inches of rain from Hurricane Frances and now more rain! Everyone was wondering how the ground would be able to hold all of the additional rain. The local weather forecasters were calling for an inch of rain from Ivan, but oh were they wrong!

As Elizabeth, a schoolteacher, left for work that morning, the rain had started to fall. It was a torrential downpour that looked as though it would not end. The rain continued all day. Finally, the principal's voice came over the loud speaker and announced that due to the rainfall, flooding was occurring so school would be dismissed early. As the students cheered, Elizabeth got an eerie feeling.

Elizabeth's home was located near a creek and although she

and her husband were assured that it would never get a "creek flood," she was worried. On the drive home she saw that water was everywhere. It was pouring off of the hillsides like faucets in a sink and some of the roads looked like rivers. As she pulled into her driveway she saw that the water had risen into her yard. Elizabeth was thankful that her husband had kept the family dogs in the house that day.

When she got into the house she called her husband to tell him the conditions of the creek. It was rising fast! After speaking to him and trying to persuade him to come home from work early, she went down to the basement and started to carry items up to safety.

Elizabeth was only able to get her children's personal items out of the basement before it started to fill up with water. Before she knew it the water was up to the ceiling of the basement. She and her husband looked in horror as their belongings floated in their basement. She watched as all the Christmas decorations, washer and dryer, freezer, couch, exercise equipment and everything else was destroyed.

Elizabeth called her sons who attended a nearby college just to make sure that they were safe. Both boys wanted to come home to help clean up the mess, but all roads were closed. She told them to stay at school until the roads reopened.

As she and her husband looked out of their dining room window they saw homes floating through their yard. The water was still rising. She and her husband had quickly packed a few things in a bag and gathered their personal papers just in case they had to evacuate. Elizabeth was listening to her police scanner and could hear which roads were closed due to the flooding and landslides. Luckily their road was still open. They loaded everything in the cars as a precaution. Then the news…their road was now closed. They were stranded! Her husband just kept saying, "Don't worry, God will get us though this…He will protect us." She knew he was right, but she couldn't help but worry.

They spent the night listening to the water slosh around in the basement…just a few inches below their feet. Elizabeth fell asleep wondering what tomorrow would bring.

The next morning the sun was shining brightly and it showed all the destruction that occurred the day before. The family discovered the extent of the damage to the home and property. The water had surrounded their home in a horseshoe-like shape and debris was everywhere.

The water from the flooded creek had started to recede and a few roads had reopened, but there was more bad news. A volunteer firefighter stopped to check on them and to tell them that more flooding was expected because the Ohio River had not yet reached its expected crest. Their only hope now was that the creek would recede enough so that the house could withstand another round of flooding.

The river did rise, but thankfully had little effect on the already flooded basement. Once all the water had gone down the real damage was realized.

Mud as thick as three inches covered everything. The couch, refrigerator, washing machine and dryer were all turned upside down and piled on top of each other. Elizabeth just stared in bewilderment at the destruction. Where to start in the cleanup?

Just then she heard cars pull into her driveway. She went to the door and saw four carloads of young men with buckets, mops, gloves, and boots. The young men were fraternity brothers of her sons and wanted to help in the cleanup effort. The young men were members of the Sigma Nu and Phi Kappa Tau fraternities.

They told Elizabeth that they wanted to help her family. The boys marched down to the basement and began cleaning up. While they were working another car pulled into the driveway, this time it was a friend of Elizabeth's, Melody, who brought cleaning supplies, food and water. The help just kept coming.

The next few days the family received help in many ways. Friends gave food, water, and even money to help Elizabeth and her family. She couldn't believe the outpouring of love and support that just kept coming.

What touched Elizabeth the most was the help from total strangers like the two fraternities who came from the nearby college, the men who drove along the road just to see what they could do to help, and then there were those who handed out cleaning supplies and some bottled water. Elizabeth and her family wondered how they could ever repay all of the acts of kindness. So many people helped them in many different ways. Although the family had gone through a tragedy, Elizabeth felt very blessed. She was thankful for all those who helped them and thankful that the flood was not worse. She still had her house, but most importantly she still had her family.

There were many Undercover Angels in this story. One would expect a "true friend" to help in a crisis situation such as a flood, but it is hard to imagine that a total stranger would stop and offer to help in the cleanup effort. What happened in this story is a true testament to the goodness of man…neighbor helping neighbor or in this case stranger helping stranger. What would the world be like if this was an everyday event…neighbor helping neighbor and stranger helping stranger…instead of just when a tragedy occurs?

The message that the Undercover Angels are spreading is that we do need to help one another all the time not just during a tragedy. We need to let our neighbors know that God is with them always and just like the footprints in the sand He carries us during the troubled times. We need to let God into our lives…we need to open our hearts and invite Him in.

"And let us consider how we may encourage one another on toward love and good deeds" (Hebrews 10:24).

Chapter 9
The Cart

IT HAD BEEN A LONG HARD day at the mill and Tony couldn't wait to get home to just sit and relax while watching the Pittsburgh Steelers on the television. As he pulled out onto the highway his cell phone rang. It was his wife asking him to pick up some chicken on the way home. Tony really didn't want to make any stops along the way…he just wanted to get home, but he reluctantly agreed.

He pulled into the parking lot of the Chicken Shak. The line in the takeout section went clear to the back of the store. *Oh great,* Tony thought, *I'm gonna miss the kickoff!* People filtered in and out and the line never seemed to move any. Finally, it was Tony's turn to place his order. After standing in line for twenty minutes he was back in his truck ready to head home. He turned the radio on so he could at least listen to the game.

Suddenly, there was a knock on his driver's side window. It was an elderly woman who was pushing a cart with some groceries and other odds and ends. Tony didn't want to be bothered but he rolled his window down and asked the woman what she wanted. She asked him if the bus stop was near and then said she thought she might be lost. It was getting dark and for some reason Tony seemed to forget about the Steelers. He heard the panic in her voice and noticed that her hands were shaking and knew he needed to help her.

Tony told the woman that the bus stop was a few blocks away, but if she told him her address he would take her home. She said that she didn't want to inconvenience him, but Tony insisted. He helped her into his truck and placed her cart in the bed of his truck. Just then a wheel from the front of the cart broke off. Tony felt terrible. He thought he would wait until he got her home before he said anything and then maybe he could fix it while he was there.

The woman could smell the chicken he had just picked up. "Oh, I am taking you away from your dinner…your family will be angry with me," she said. "Don't worry about it, your house is on the way," Tony answered. It really wasn't on the way, but he didn't want to make her feel uneasy about accepting the ride home.

As the truck pulled in front of her house, Tony saw an elderly gentleman sitting on a rocking chair on the front porch. He was smoking a pipe and rings of smoke seemed to form a halo around the man's head. The man started to walk down to meet them as if her knew Tony would be bringing his wife home. When he reached the truck, Tony told him that she was looking for the bus stop and was lost so he offered her a ride home. He also apologized for breaking the wheel off the cart and even offered to fix it. She told him that he shouldn't worry about it because they were just "flimsy plastic ones" and that the wheel was always breaking.

By now the man had introduced himself as her husband, Seth. While she walked up to the porch, he told Tony how much he appreciated the help he gave his wife. Then Seth told him that his wife had the beginnings of Alzheimer's disease and that she was also legally blind. Tony didn't know what to say. He just shook Seth's hand and got in his truck and headed home.

As he drove home he thought about what might have happened to her if he had not offered to give her a ride home. He wondered if someone else would have helped her.

When he got home he explained to his wife what had happened and how the plastic wheel on the cart broke. Just then his wife got an eerie look on her face and left the table. She walked in the garage and opened the van door.

Tony was wondering what his wife was doing and why he had such a strange look on her face. Just then she entered the dining pushing a cart that she bought at the flea market that morning. It had metal wheels! She told Tony she had no idea why she bought it. "Something just made me buy it!" she pleaded. Then they noticed that a name had been etched into the handle. It read "Kate M."

Tony and his wife knew what they had to do...they had to give the cart to the old woman. So they loaded the cart in the truck and took it over that night. As they drove up to the house they noticed a single light was shining through the front window. Tony parked the truck and took the cart from the truck bed. Slowly he walked up the front stairs and reached for the doorbell, but Seth had heard the footsteps and met Tony at the door.

Tony apologized for coming to the house so late. Then he wheeled the cart to the door and told Seth that it was a replacement for the cart that was broken earlier in the day. Tony expressed regret that it wasn't new, but explained how his wife had bought the cart earlier in the day at the flea market. Then Tony showed the man the name that was etched into the cart's handle.

Seth just stood there...he didn't say a word. Seth finally broke the silence and told Tony that his wife's name was Kate. He told

Tony how he was at the flea market that morning selling some of their belongings and that Tony's wife must have been the one to buy the cart. He said he had to sell the cart and some of their other belongings so that he could buy Kate's medicine. By now, Kate had come to the door and when she saw the cart she couldn't quit smiling.

Tony pushed the cart to her and said that apparently God didn't want anyone else to have it but Kate. With that she looked at him, gave him a big hug, and asked, "Are you my angel?" Tony just smiled, shook Seth's hand and walked back to the truck.

When he got into his truck, Tony got a "warm and fuzzy" feeling as he explained the whole scenario to his wife. They both smiled because they knew that they had done a good deed. Then Tony's wife said, "I wonder if this was in God's plan."

What would have happened if Tony didn't take the time to help Kate or what if his wife didn't listen to that "something" that made her buy the cart. They may never know what impact that small gesture of kindness and act of love did for that elderly couple.

The "warm and fuzzy" feeling Tony had was really a "pat on the back" from God...His "thank you" for taking care of His children and welcoming him to the Undercover Angels. God used both Tony and his wife as an instrument to help an elderly couple in their time of need.

God uses many different types of instruments to help us in our lives. Have you had a "warm and fuzzy" feeling after helping another person? Was that God talking to you? He speaks to us often...we just need to listen, but not just with our ears, but also with our hearts.

"So when you give to the needy, do not announce it with trumpets, as the hypocrites do in the synagogues and on the streets, to be honored by men. I tell you the truth; they have received their reward in full. But when you give to the needy, do not let your left hand know what your right hand is doing" (Matthew 6:2).

Chapter 10
The Note

IT WAS A RAINY FEBRUARY EVENING and Linda's husband, Sam, was due home from work anytime. As the hours passed by, Linda got a strange feeling that something was terribly wrong. Just then the phone rang and Linda somehow knew it was about Sam.

The gentleman on the other end introduced himself as a deputy sheriff and informed her that Sam had been arrested for driving on a suspended license. Linda felt everything go numb. Then she asked the officer to explain what he meant by "suspended license."

"Your husband had his license revoked from a past DUI. He is not to be driving," the officer said.

"I never knew he had a DUI…when did this happened?' Linda asked sheepishly.

"The DUI occurred in 1997 and it was a second offense. His license has been revoked for a period of ten years," replied the deputy.

The deputy then explained the process that Linda would have to take to make bail for her husband. As she listened to the steps involved, Linda just sat at the table devastated feeling as though her world and family was falling apart. This was all new to her… she never had to get anyone out of jail before. The deputy then told her that she would receive a call the following morning with more details and a specific time to pick up her husband.

Linda could hardly sleep that night. She kept asking herself one question: "Who is this man that I am married to?" She couldn't help but wonder what else he may be hiding from her. Although the DUI came a year before they met, Linda thought that it was something she should have been told about. She doubted that it would have changed her feelings for him then, but now was a different story.

The next morning, around nine o'clock, the phone rang. It was Sam…he told her to pick him up at the regional jail and gave her directions to the location. She wrote them down on the notepad that she kept on the refrigerator door.

"I am sorry, honey, but everything is going to be okay," Sam said. "They let me out with no bail so you just need to come and get me."

"Why didn't you tell me about your license and the DUI?" Linda said, her voice now quivering. "Is there anything else in your closet that I should know about?" she asked as tears streamed down her face.

Sam told her he would explain everything when she came to pick him up. As she hung up the phone she tore the note from the notepad. She stared at the next slip of paper on the pad. It had a note written in it. As she read that note the tears came faster and harder down her cheeks. The note said, "I love you very much…Hang in there! It will be OK…Love you, Mom."

Her mother-in-law, Anne, wrote the note while she was visiting them for Christmas. Linda couldn't believe that on a day that she needed a "pick me up" she got one that was written almost two months ago. It was perfect timing!

Linda picked up the phone and called her mother-in-law to let her know that she had just received the note and how appropriate it was that it came that day. She explained the whole situation to Anne and thanked her for writing the "love note." It was apparent to Linda that it was a sign from God that everything would work out; she just needed to be patient.

The drive to the regional jail seemed long and many thoughts went through Linda's head, but all thoughts kept bringing her back to the note. How ironic that something that was written in December would appear on a day that Linda needed it the most.

As she pulled into the parking lot of the jail, her husband came out and got into the car. "We have a few things to talk about," Linda said. "Is there anything else about you I should know about?"

"No," Sam replied. "I know I should have told you about the DUI from the beginning, but I was embarrassed by it and thought what you didn't know wouldn't hurt."

"Well, it did hurt!" snapped Linda. "I don't know who you are anymore!"

Sam turned and looked out the window. He didn't know what to say. Neither spoke another word until they reached the driveway. "You don't seem as angry as I thought you would be," Sam said calmly.

"I found a note from your mother and it kinda changed my outlook on things. It made me more calm and gave me ah…ah…hug," Linda replied.

"How can a note give a hug?" Sam asked.

Then Linda explained how she found the note his mother left on the refrigerator door notepad. Sam couldn't believe that his mother picked at random a paper in the middle of the pad and of all days, it surfaced today.

When they got out of the car, Sam walked over to Linda and wrapped his arms around her. She looked at him and told him that she was still angry, but knew that things would work out in the end. When Sam asked how she knew that, Linda said that the note from his mother wasn't a coincidence; it was a message from God that although things may get rough, they would be fine. They just needed to have faith and believe. Sam smiled, held Linda tight, and thanked God for the things in his life.

Imagine getting a note from someone hundreds of miles away that was written two months prior that fit that very day's events. God the Father does work in mysterious ways. He leaves us "love notes" all the time; we just have to take the time to read them. How would Sam's mother, Anne, know that what she wrote while visiting her son and his family would be read on a day that the family needed reassurance the most.

Anne was a recruit in the Army of God. Her note was the instrument that was used to help a wounded heart. What if she never wrote it? Would Linda have been as forgiving or would she have turned a wounded heart into a cold heart? A marriage and a family could have been ruined had that note not been written.

Satan is out to destroy marriages and split families. He had Linda and Sam in his sights, but the Almighty Father crushed his plan not with a sword, but with a simple ballpoint pen. The smallest action does indeed have the biggest impact!

"You are my refuge and my shield; I have put my hope in your word" (Psalms 119:114).

Chapter 11
Help from Within

SOMETIMES HELP AND COMFORT CAN COME from an unlikely source and we know that God uses whomever He chooses to do His work. This is a story about George, the head of maintenance at the local high school.

George had an exceptional rapport with the special education students in the high school. He would sometimes come into the classroom and check on the students' behavior and academic progress. He would tell them that he expected them to do their classwork and get good grades. George took an active interest in these students and would help their teacher in any way that he could. One could tell that these students and their teacher thought highly of him.

One day, Keith, a special education student with severe emotional problems, ran out of classroom. The teacher was unable to leave the room to chase after him, so she sent a student to the office to report the incident. George, who was helping to unload a truck, saw Keith leave the building.

George yelled for Keith to stop, but the boy started to run and that was when the chase began. George ran after Keith and followed him through the parking lot and down into a gully. Keith thought that he could hide under the old trestle bridge, but George soon found him.

What happened next dumbfounded Keith. George walked up and sat down beside him. He didn't give a lecture or a long talk…he just asked him "what was going on?" The two talked for a long time. Keith did most of the talking and George just listened. The boy kept saying how he hated high school and was going to quit. When Keith finished, George gave his opinion of the situation.

"You are going to graduate in two months…why give up now?" George asked. "You put up with it for almost four years, why quit now…you are almost finished?"

Keith didn't really give a response to those remarks. He just got up and started walking back to the high school. When they reached the classroom, George told the teacher what had happened and how he had a talk with Keith.

"Everything should be okay, now…we had a long talk," George said.

When the teacher asked him what the talk was about, George told her that it was between the young boy and him. As George turned to leave the room, Keith looked up at him and smiled. It was as if he was telling George, "Thanks for caring."

It was late May now and all the seniors were gathered in the hallway waiting to make their entrance into the gymnasium. It was graduation day! Standing there in the line was Keith, wearing his green cap and gown. George walked up to him and shook his hand and congratulated him for staying in school and reaching this milestone. Keith thanked George for his support and for being there when he needed someone to listen…he thanked him for caring about him. Then Keith turned, got in line and walked into the gymnasium with the rest the graduates.

Because Keith now had a high school diploma, he was able to get a job at a local restaurant. He became a productive citizen in society. Would he have been able to do this without someone like George who cared and listened to his problems rather than pass judgment on him?

George is not unique in his caring and love for people, but he went a step farther than just talking about helping others, he actually practiced that belief. God used George to reach out to Keith when he needed help. George helps anyone who is in need regardless of who they are. He is a true Undercover Angel, but he would be the first to tell you that he isn't, he is just doing what is right! He lives the Golden Rule of Christianity: "*Do onto others as you would wish them done onto you.*"

"By this all will know that you are My disciples, if you have love for one another" (John 13:35).

Chapter 12
Hell for Eternity

MOST OF US DON'T KNOW WHAT it is like to be plagued by demons or to hear demonic voices, but there are some people who live that life every day. This story touches on that subject and how one unsuspecting woman changed the life of a young man.

Sally was a new teacher in the school district. She was excited about her assignment as a history teacher in the local high school. She would be teaching American History II and World History I. Sally had students from all grades 9-12. Most students came from the lower middle class, but there were a few from the poverty level. The school district is in a rural steel mill town in the rolling hills of West Virginia on the banks of the mighty Ohio River.

As the school year progressed, Sally began to see a drastic change in Tyler. Once a steady "B" student, his grades dropped to an alarming "D" and since he was a senior she knew he needed the credit to graduate. Sally noticed that along with the changes in his grades, Tyler's mode of dress went to the "gothic" style. He would come to class dressed in black from head to toe and now had the "I hate school" attitude. She noticed that he had a new set of friends and heard that he quit the wrestling team. She became more concerned and spoke with the guidance counselor.

When speaking with the guidance counselor, Sally found that she was not the only teacher to express concern for Tyler and that his parents were called to convey those concerns. While speaking to his parents, the counselor discovered that Tyler's mother found a notebook of his that was filled with expressions of suicide. The parents didn't know where to turn so they called to school for advice.

The guidance counselor recommended that they seek mental help for Tyler and that they monitor him at all times. The guidance counselor had "suicide training," so she spoke to all teachers concerning the signs of suicide and what to look for when someone is contemplating an act such as: talking about death, giving one's possessions away, or withdrawing from friends and family. After meeting with the teachers the principal then spoke and stated that under no circumstances should any staff member refer Tyler to any religious counseling…"We are a public school…no religion!" stated the principal.

Tyler's parents contacted the school after a few days and informed them that Tyler was scheduled for psychological testing at a local mental hospital. When the results were known, the doctors would advise the school as to the findings.

When the testing was completed the hospital administrator spoke to the parents concerning admitting Tyler for psychiatric help for a period of thirty days. The administrator told his parents that Tyler informed the evaluator that he was hearing voices that kept telling him to kill himself. Tyler even said that the voices came from hell and although he was afraid of them…he wanted to do what they said. Tyler's parents agreed to the thirty-day stay. They were hoping that it would bring back the "old" Tyler.

The school was notified about the situation and the teachers were to send work once a week so that Tyler would be caught up when he returned. The staff at the high school seemed relived that Tyler would be getting the necessary help.

Then two weeks later, Tyler arrives at school with his parents. Apparently, the hospital released Tyler because the insurance wouldn't pay for a thirty-day stay. So his parents had to take him to an outpatient program twice a week at the hospital. Now the teachers and school staff were back on the "suicide watch."

As Tyler came to class a few days later, Sally noticed that he had been crying. So, she wrote the day's assignment on the board and as the other students began their work, she went to speak to Tyler. Sally sat next to Tyler and spoke in a soft quiet voice and asked what had happened. What he said to her shook this new teacher to the core!

"I hear the voices telling me to do bad things and now I am seeing them!" Tyler murmured through his tears. Now Sally knew that the guidance counselor was out for the day and she didn't want to pass this off especially since Tyler was speaking about it, so she pressed him for more information.

"What are they saying, Tyler?" Sally asked.

Tyler replied, "They are telling me that they want me to be with them because nobody likes me." Tyler's voice was getting louder now and most of the students were paying more attention to the conversation than to their work. "I see them now…they are so ugly…they won't leave me alone…they tell me God doesn't love me!"

Then Sally took a chance, she asked Tyler, "Do you like school, Tyler?"

"No!" he exclaimed, "I hate it!"

"Well, Tyler, I believe in God and I know that God loves you and doesn't want you to listen to those voices. You see, if you kill yourself then you will go to hell with all those ugly demons that you have been seeing." She went on, "And hell is a place where we are surrounded by the things that we hate most of all and since you hate this high school, then your hell will be high school for eternity!" Sally told him.

Tyler looked at her and, wiping a tear from his eyes, said, "High school for eternity...I couldn't handle that!"

Sally also told Tyler that if he changed his ways and turned to God for help, then the demons and their voices would go away.

"Give it a try, Tyler...you have nothing to lose! You will either graduate from here in a few months and be free from the 'high school' or you will be with us for eternity...you make the call!" Sally told him. "Frankly, I would prefer to graduate and move on to something bigger and better, but if you want to be in my class forever...well—"

Tyler interrupted her, "I don't want to be here forever...maybe I will talk to my minister."

As the bell for the end of class rang, Tyler got up and hugged Sally and thanked her for caring. When he left the classroom, Sally walked to the principal's office and told him about the events. She thought for sure that he would have her fired, but instead he told her to report the incident to the guidance counselor the next morning and also to inform Tyler's parents.

A few months later, during the graduation ceremonies, Tyler's parents came up to thank Sally for helping their son. He had indeed sought counseling from his minister and was making progress in his outpatient therapy. When the parents asked her what exactly she said that made a difference in their son's outlook, Sally said that she told him that if he killed himself then he would go to hell and that hell was the high school for eternity! She also explained that she didn't know why she said that..."*it just came out!*"

Sally risked her job by speaking to Tyler about God, but her belief that all life is precious and had worth compelled her to speak of her conviction. God used Sally as an instrument to reach and save Tyler. God spoke through Sally to Tyler's heart...Tyler heard the message and felt the arms of our Heavenly Father envelop him…he finally felt safe and loved, but it wasn't an earthly love, but rather a spiritual love.

Tyler visited his old high school a few years later and went to see Sally while she was on her planning period. He thanked her for saving his life…his very soul. He was thinking about going to college to become a youth counselor and maybe even into youth ministry.

Where would Tyler be today if Sally hadn't spoken to him about her belief? How many of us would have left him alone that afternoon and just recorded his behavior. Sally was the Undercover Angel sent by God to rescue Tyler in his hour of need.

> "If anyone speaks, he should do it as one speaking the very words of God. If anyone serves, he should do it with the strength God provides, so that in all things God may be praised through Jesus Christ. To Him be the glory and power forever and ever, Amen" (1 Peter 4:11).

Chapter 13
The Messenger

THERE ARE TIMES THAT WE HEAR God speaking to us, but we choose not to listen to what He is saying. The Almighty Father asks us to do His work every day, but there are many times that we turn a deaf ear because what is asked of us may be a difficult task.

In this story, we find that Becca, a dedicated Christian woman, received a message from God that she was to deliver to another. Becca wasn't sure how she was to complete this task, but knew that she had to follow God's will.

She had had the same dream for a week now. In this dream she was given a message from God that she was to pass along to a gentleman she had never seen before. Although she did not know this man he was present in every dream and the message was always the same, "There is a New Age Conference at the hotel next door and we need to pray about it."

Becca wasn't sure why she was having the dream...although

she was familiar with the New Age movement, there was nothing going on in her life that even touched on that topic. After a week of the same dream reoccurring, she realized that it was a message from God. But what exactly was its meaning?

A few days later as Becca was reading the local newspaper, she read about a conference coming to a neighboring city. The conference was going to be held during the coming weekend and its topic was "The New Age Movement." As Becca read the story she got chills over her whole body. Becca knew that the New Age belief was that God and humankind are actually one, a concept it calls monism (one-ism). She also knew that some view this movement as a cult, but it is more than that…it was Satanic in origin and those who practice this New Age Movement dabble in the consulting of spirit mediums, horoscopes, tarot cards, and predicting the future.

Becca knew now what her dream had meant and that she was to pass God's message on to the person in her dream. As the days passed she was more aware of the people around her as she was looking for the individual from her dream.

While she was having lunch with her pastor and his wife, she saw the gentleman from her dream. There sitting in the booth across from her was an older man having lunch with his wife. Becca felt that if she told this man he would think she was crazy. She resisted passing the message on.

When Becca went to the salad bar…he was there right beside her and she didn't say a word. Then at the dessert bar he was there again and she still couldn't tell him. Becca actually walked out of the restaurant and never passed God's message on, but because God works in wondrous ways, Becca had to return to the restaurant because she left her purse. She recognized that she didn't forget her purse by accident…it was God telling her to complete the task assigned to her. As she walked to the table she stopped at the gentleman's table and told him, "I am not real sure what this means, but God wanted me to tell you that there is a

New Age Conference at the hotel next door and that we need to pray for those people attending this event and for those who are promoting it."

Becca thought for sure that the man would think she was crazy, but instead he thanked her and said that he would have his congregation pray for them during their Sunday service. He proceeded to tell Becca that he was a pastor at the local Methodist Church and he appreciated the fact that she relayed the message to him.

When Becca walked out of the restaurant, she thanked God for giving her the opportunity to do His work and asked forgiveness for having second thoughts about delivering His message.

Becca is an example of hearing God's message and heeding to His will. How many of us would have thought the dream a fluke and not understood its meaning? God works through us every minute of every day...sometimes we recognize his works and sometimes they go unnoticed. What would have happened if Becca chose not to speak to the man and relay God's message? God wanted to have as many people as possible pray for those who are misled into believing in the New Age Movement. This is just an example of how God loves all of us, not just the believers, but the unbelievers as well and he wants us all to join Him in Heaven.

This is just an illustration of what measures the Lord will take to bring us all Home to Him in Heaven. He encourages all of us to pray for each other and love each other unconditionally no matter what our differences may be. Becca was the vessel that God chose to use so that His message of Love would reach as many unbelievers as possible. Becca was not a "recruited" Undercover Angel, but rather she was a willing "volunteer," who opened her heart to the Lord God. By letting God into her life, Becca was really saying, *"Lord, I am indeed Your servant"* (Psalm 116:16).

Her one moment of weakness and doubt about delivering the

message was the work of Satan. He was trying to prevent Becca from doing God's work. Satan is always looking for ways to get us off track and to divert us from the Lord God. That is why the Lord sent the Undercover Angels to us, so that we will not battle Satan and his demonic spirits single-handedly. Because we cannot fight evil alone, if we try we will surely lose, but with the help of the Undercover Angels, whose power comes from God, we will be triumphant and have our place among the saints and angels in Heaven.

Becca gave herself to God unselfishly like a little child. She trusted in the Lord completely. For it is written in the Bible, "*I tell you the truth, anyone who will not receive the kingdom of God like a little child will never enter it*" (Mark 10:15).

Chapter 14
The Yard Sale

SHIRLEY HAD GONE THROUGH HER HOUSE with a fine-tooth comb collecting items for her annual yard sale. She had plenty of goodies for this year's sale. During the weeks that led up to the sale Shirley was busy making sure that all of the items were cleaned and priced.

There was an abundance of baby clothes and toys from her daughter's closet and she couldn't wait to get rid of the red glassware that her mother-in-law had given them last year. As the date drew near, Shirley had everything organized. All of the signs were posted and she even put an ad in the local newspaper.

At seven a.m. on that Saturday morning she was putting the last-minute touches on the beautifully displayed items. The toys were on the far table next to the baby clothes, then there were the adult clothes, and her husband's sporting equipment that he just couldn't live without but never used and finally household items.

The people started to come early and the crowd never really

seemed to thin out until two p.m. She had sold most of the wares and was getting tired and ready to call it a day when a young woman with her little blonde-haired girl stopped by.

Shirley could tell that they had very little and the little girl went right to the remaining toys and started to play while her mother reviewed the remnants of the clothing. The young woman was gathering some clothing in her arms and the little girl selected some of the toys and handed them to her mother who in turn handed them to Shirley. As Shirley bagged and totaled up the purchase she was amazed that it filled two garbage bags full of clothing for the little girl and her mother. The toys filled another bag!

Shirley informed the young mother that the total for the clothing and the toys would be ten dollars. She had actually cut the price in half because she knew they were so poor. The young woman asked Shirley if she could hold the items while she walked home and got more money. The woman informed her that she lived at the other end of town and it would take her about a half an hour before she returned. Now Shirley knew that the woman could never carry all the bags and hold on to her daughter, so she offered to ride the woman and her daughter home.

The young mother smiled broadly and accepted instantly. Shirley loaded everything into her car and drove the small family home. When the young mother unloaded her yard sale purchases from the car, she told Shirley she would return to the car to give her the money. After about ten minutes of waiting, Shirley realized that she would never see that money and that her good deed of driving them home probably made her a laughing stock in that neighborhood.

As Shirley drove off she just said a little prayer for that young woman and thanked God that she was able to at least ensure that the little girl had some clothing. Shirley thought that maybe this young woman didn't have any money and was just too proud to admit it.

When she arrived home she told her neighbors what had happened. One of her neighbors was a police officer, who after hearing the description of the young woman, informed Shirley that this woman was known as a "panhandler" and that she had been in jail for numerous offenses of fraud. Apparently, this young woman uses the appearance of being in need to con people out of their money and goods. He told Shirley that she had been this woman's latest victim and that she should file a complaint against her.

She didn't really care that she was "conned" because in her heart she knew she was doing the right thing by helping someone who was less fortunate. Shirley didn't mind that the woman had taken advantage of her good heart because what items weren't sold would have been given to the Salvation Army, anyway. She did object to the fact that the little girl was being used as a "heartstrings tugger" so that the sneaky objective could be achieved.

Shirley was a victim of a "user," someone who takes advantage of the kindness of others and exploits them. Shirley did exactly what God wants us to do. She was taking care of the poor and less fortunate. Although she never received payment for her yard sale things, Shirley felt a sense of happiness knowing that her good deed would not go unnoticed by God. She did ask the Father to help the young mother see the errors of her ways and repent. She also asked for special care for the little child so that she may not grow up in the lifestyle of lies and deception.

The Father sees all that we do and all that we don't do. He knows our hearts and He knew that the young woman was going to take advantage of Shirley, but He also knew Shirley's heart and saw that she was willing to help the family any way that she could. Shirley could have easily told the woman to go get the money first and then return to pick up her purchases, but she was trying to help. This incident with the "user" has not stopped Shirley from helping others. She continues to this day reaching out to anyone who is in need.

"Let your light shine before men, that they may see your good deeds and praise your Father in heaven" (Matthew 5:16)

Chapter 15
Milk Bottles

THE YEAR WAS 1924 AND SIX-YEAR-OLD Emily was getting ready to start school the very next day. Her mother, Clara, had sent Emily to the store to buy two pints of milk. As the little girl skipped down the street she recited her ABC's, she had been practicing them all summer.

When Emily arrived at Ganion's Market she spoke to the elderly gentlemen sitting outside playing a game of checkers. She walked inside the store and told the store clerk, Miss Emma, that she was to buy two pints of milk. With a smile on her face, Miss Emma walked over to the cooler and took out the pints of milk. She asked Emily if she was ready to start school the next day and commented on what a big girl she was now. Emily just smiled and paid Miss Emma for the milk.

As Emily walked out of the store, her foot caught on the step and she went tumbling down the porch stairs. The bottles broke spilling milk all over the stairs. The people nearby just stood in shock as they watched the blood pour out of Emily's right arm.

She had cut an artery in her arm and was bleeding profusely. Everyone seemed to be moving in slow motion and Emily was lying there in a daze. She could hear a woman yelling to go get her mother, but no one seemed to be rushing to her side. Then suddenly Charlie, the local handyman, came from out of the crowd and picked up Emily.

Charlie carried Emily to one of the town's local doctors, but the office was closed. Emily could hear Charlie say, "You jus' hold on, child. Uncle Charlie gonna git you help."

Emily knew Uncle Charlie because he was the nice black man that always helped out at Ganion's Market. She remembered that her daddy said that Uncle Charlie was a hard worker who helps everyone in town.

As Charlie turned away from the closed doctor's office he ran right into Emily's mother. Clara heard someone yell that there was a new doctor in town and his office was just around the next corner.

The blood was running down Emily's arm and had covered Charlie's shirt. He was almost running now to get Emily the help she needed. When he arrived at the office Charlie yelled for someone to open the door. As the doctor opened the door he saw what the emergency was all about. He motioned for Charlie to put Emily on the table.

The doctor asked Charlie what had happened just as Clara made her way into the office. They informed the doctor that Emily had fallen while carrying the glass milk bottles. As the doctor examined the cut, which went from Emily's wrist to her elbow, he saw that she had indeed cut an artery. While he stitched up her arm, Charlie slipped out of the office without being noticed.

By now Emily's father, Henry, had arrived at the office. Clara told him what had happened and how Charlie had saved their little girl. After Emily was bandaged up, the doctor agreed with

Clara, "Your daughter would have bled to death if he hadn't acted when he did."

Now Henry went out to look for Charlie and found him at the local bar. He thanked him for saving Emily and asked if there was any way to repay him for his act. Charlie just smiled and said that knowing that she was all right was payment enough.

Charlie was an Undercover Angel for Emily. He saved her life when it seemed other people just stood there and did nothing. What if he didn't step forward to help? How long would the people have let Emily lay there until someone, if anyone, stepped in to help? Charlie made a great decision that day. He chose to help another…to save a life of a stranger.

He took the path that the Undercover Angels led him to take, but Charlie didn't stay on that path. Just a few months later he was arrested for the murder of his wife.

How could someone who saved the life of a stranger a few months earlier turn around and willingly take the life of a loved one? Charlie went from the path of goodness to a sinful course in life. Even those who choose to be an Undercover Angel can be tempted to fall away from God's Grace. No one is perfect or without sin. We must make a conscious effort every day to remain true to God's values and His message.

"But as for you, continue in what you have learned and have become convinced of, because you know those from whom you learned it, and how from infancy you have known the holy Scriptures which are able to make you wise for salvation through faith in Christ Jesus" (2 Timothy 3:14).

Chapter 16
The Neighborhood Nurse

HELEN LIVED WITH HER ELDERLY PARENTS, Harry and Polly. She never married because her passion in life was being a nurse. Helen loved taking care of others. She would always visit the people in her small community when they were ill. Helen would administer their insulin or B12 shots. She would make sure that all of the medication was up to date and that they went for regular doctor's visits.

Helen, a Catholic, faithfully attended daily mass. She would go to church either before work or after work…she never missed a day. On Sunday mornings she could be found in the front pew at church sitting with her parents. After church Helen would go visiting friends and family bringing home baked cookies, cakes, or pies wherever she stopped. She always had a smile on her face. If there were organizations around town that needed someone to help…she would always volunteer. Helen was someone everyone knew they could count on. She loved helping people! She was known throughout the town as the "neighborhood nurse."

"When God's children are in need, be the one to help them out" (Romans 12:13).

Then during one evening the telephones began ringing throughout the town. The news spread that Helen, their neighborhood nurse, had been rushed to the local hospital. Soon people began gathering at the church. The people, who came from many denominations, began an impromptu ecumenical prayer service.

She had been home making cookies for the Methodist Church Youth Group's Valentine's Day bake sale. Her mother heard a loud thud come from the kitchen and called out to see if Helen was all right. Helen didn't reply, so her mother walked into the kitchen and found Helen lying on the floor.

It wasn't long before another call came in…Helen had died. She had a massive heart attack. The people of her community were devastated. Helen's death hit the community and her family quite hard. Now the neighbors, who were once being taken care of by her, were now taking care of her parents.

The next day during the Sunday sermon the priest did his best to explain God's reason for calling Helen home. Then he reminded the people that the day she died was February 14, Valentine's Day…a day that honors "Love." He went on to say how ironic and yet fitting that Helen had died on that day because she had a true love for everyone and that she touched many lives with her kindness.

That evening as the family was finalizing all of Helen's funeral arrangements, the telephone rang. It was Father York calling to say that the plaster from the church ceiling had collapsed onto the floor and the interior of the church had been damaged. He informed them that Helen's funeral would have to be held at the Catholic Church in a neighboring town. There was not enough time to call a construction company for help in removing the debris and to make the necessary repairs to the church. Helen's parents, who were already distraught, sat there frozen. They desperately wanted their daughter to be buried out of the church that she attended all of her life.

Again the phones across town began to ring. This time the people, numbering close to one hundred, went to the church not to pray but to clean up the mess that had been left from the fallen plaster. The people stayed overnight and into the next day clearing away the debris. Damaged pews were carried out and replaced with folding chairs donated from the many churches across town. The townspeople wanted to ensure that the church was ready for Helen's funeral.

On February 17 Helen was buried from the church that had been her spiritual home all of her life. The number of people who came to say goodbye to their "neighbor nurse" seemed endless. The church was packed with people of all faiths to pay respect to a woman who made a difference in their lives.

The people came together to help a grieving family bury a loved one, but also the people were helping themselves during the grieving process. They felt as though they were giving back to Helen what she had given them…love.

Helen was an Undercover Angel who impacted many lives. She left that "seed of love" in everyone she came into contact with and it began to grow in the people when news came of her death. In return those same people became Undercover Angels. They helped Helen's family to hold the funeral mass from the church she loved so much. Their actions of clearing away debris and cleaning the church were done from a true love. It was their way of saying "thank you" to an angel of a woman.

"If we love one another, God lives in us, and His love is made complete in us" (1 John 4:12).

Chapter 17
The Hunters

STANLEY AND HIS FAMILY WERE TRAVELING to his sister's house for Christmas Eve in 1963. His sister and her husband had just bought a new home. The directions that they gave Stanley were the long way to their home and it was the safest way. There was a short cut, but it was not advisable to travel that country road in the winter. Stanley, however, did not want to take the long way, so he chose to take his family over the country road.

After packing the Desoto with all of the presents, the family climbed into the car and left on their journey. Stanley had told his wife, Ruth, that he had found a short cut that would take at least thirty minutes off their one and half hour drive. Ruth was not particularly happy with his decision to leave the main road, especially since there was snow on the ground!

It was an unusually bitter cold December day and the news was forecasting a potential snowstorm to hit that evening. Stanley reassured his family that they would reach his sister's house well before the storm hit.

The children were singing Christmas carols in the back seat when Stanley turned off onto County Road 74. It was an unpaved road and Ruth could hear the gravel pinging against the car. The road was windy and had many different turnoffs along the way. Although they had only driven a short distance, it seemed as though they were on that road for hours. Stanley took a right and then a left…it led right to a barn! He backed out of that driveway and turned back onto the country road. As the car was traveling down the road, Stanley swerved to miss hitting a deer that jumped into the path of the Desoto. The family's car slid on the ice and went into a deep ditch along the side of the road.

The children let out a scream and packages went flying everywhere, but luckily no one was injured. Stanley climbed out of the Desoto to survey the damage to his car. As he walked around the car he saw that it had not been damaged, but it appeared to him that the car was stuck. He got back into the car and tried to rock it back and forth to free it from the ditch. Try as he might, the old Desoto was stuck.

To make matters worse it started to snow and the wind was picking up. After sitting in the car for a few minutes the family heard the sound of a motor. Soon they saw a tractor approaching them. Stanley jumped out and flagged the driver down and asked for help. The farmer backed up the tractor so that it was just a few feet from the Desoto. He took a heavy chain and fastened it to the back of his tractor and the other end to the undercarriage of the car. Then the farmer climbed on the tractor and pressed on the gas pedal as he attempted to remove the car from the ditch…the car lurched forward and the children squealed with joy.

The farmer pressed harder on the pedal and then…SNAP! The chain had broken! With a disgusted look on his face he jumped down off of the tractor to inspect the situation. Then he told Stanley he would drive on home and see what else he might have that would help them get the car out of the ditch.

As he drove off, Ruth got out of the car. "Stanley, what are we going to do? It is snowing pretty good now and the kids are getting cold?" she asked.

"We'll be okay, Ruth, the Lord is watching over us. After all, it is Christmas Eve!" Stanley said.

As the family waited in the car hoping for the farmer's quick return, it began to snow harder and the wind was whipping through the trees. The children were complaining that they were getting cold and hungry. It was almost completely dark when two shadowy figures came out of the woods and approached the car.

The men never said word as each one went to a section of the rear bumper. They motioned for the family to get out of the car. With the family standing on the side of the country road, they watched as the two men lifted the Desoto out of the ditch and pushed it onto the road. Stanley stood there speechless as he observed these men lift the heavy car onto the road. Now that the car was back on the road, the children climbed inside to get out of the cold.

One of the men then spoke and said that they were hunters and saw that the car was caught in a ditch. Neither man gave his name they just asked, "You are traveling to your sister's for Christmas Eve?" Stanley just nodded. "Then you need to go down this road for five miles and then turn right onto Mill Run Road. Her house will be the third one on the right. She is waiting for you and your family," the hunter said.

Stanley and Ruth thanked them for their help and asked what their names were and if there was any way that they could repay them. The two men wished the family well and walked back into the woods.

Stanley and Ruth stood there dumbfounded. Each one looked at the other knowing that Ginny's name was never mentioned and that neither had asked for directions.

As they got into the car Ruth asked, "Who do you think they were?"

Stanley shrugged his shoulders. "Maybe they were our Christmas angels."

When the family arrived at Stanley's sister's, Ginny ran out of the house and met them at the driveway. The children spilled out of the car and swarmed around Ginny. They were all telling her of the day's happenings. She looked at Stanley and Ruth and both nodded in agreement with the children's description of the events.

"I have been praying to God that you would arrive here safe. I asked Him to help you if you were in trouble," Ginny said as she hugged then both.

"Well, Ginny, I would have to say that He was watching out for us this evening and sent us two angels disguised as hunters," Ruth said.

Later that evening, as the family sat around the fireplace Stanley kept thinking about the two men who helped get the car back onto the road. The men were big, Stanley thought but the Desoto is an extremely heavy car...how did they lift it? He couldn't find an answer to that question, so he just thanked God that those men came to help and that his family was safe.

Stanley has never forgotten that Christmas Eve in 1963 and the strangers who came out of the woods to help him. He firmly believes that they were really angels that were sent by God to aid his family during their time of need. It left such as impact on him that from that day forward whenever he sees a motorist in need, he pulls over and offers his help. Stanley is still trying to give back to others what was given to him and his family...love.

Who were those two men? Were they really angels sent by God? The first answer would be yes! They were Undercover Angels sent by God to help a family in need. What is our proof? First, no human being could lift a car that had partially slid into a deep ditch and then place it on the road. Secondly, how did they know where the family was headed when no one mentioned the need for directions? These Undercover Angels made such an impact on Stanley that he helps anyone who is in need, but especially stranded motorists. He was recruited by these Undercover Angels to be in God's earthly army. How wonderful it is to know that the Father's army of angels is guarding us!

"For He will command His angels concerning you to guard you in all your ways, they will lift you up in their hands so that you will not strike your foot against a stone" (Psalms 91:11-12).

Chapter 18
The Choice

THE STORIES THAT YOU HAVE JUST read were actual events that took place. Most were ordinary people who answered God's call to action. They were His instruments of Love used to help His children during their time of need. All of them could have turned a deaf ear to God's calling, but instead they listened with their spiritual ear, their heart, and followed His wishes. All of us struggle with the daily temptations that Satan has placed in our path. We must make our decisions carefully and rely on God for help.

> "Do not offer the parts of your body to sin, as instruments of wickedness, but rather offer yourselves to God, as those who have been brought from death to life; and offer the parts of your body to Him as instruments of righteousness" (Romans 6:13).

Our life is like a tree and our paths are like branches, some of our "branches" are straighter than others. God knows what the outcomes are at the end of each "branch" and he wants our tree of life to flourish. We may choose to take the path that looks the straightest and easiest to travel, but that may not always be the wisest of decisions.

Sometimes the branches that are the most crooked bear the best fruit. Just because something seems easy does not mean it is good for us physically, emotionally, or spiritually. We must rely on the gardeners of life, the Undercover Angels, to help us on our walk. They use God's love as their "miracle grow" to help our branches bear good fruit and to clear our path of the weeds that would suck the very life from our roots…our soul.

Our war with Satan began the day we were conceived in our mother's womb and will end upon our death. The battle rages constantly and our souls are the spoils of this war. Their destination is either the reward or the sentence. The choice is ours.

The Angels of the Lord use their swords that were forged in the fires of Honesty, Compassion, Truth, and Love to shield us from the evil advances of Satan. But evil uses the weapons of Deceit, Deception, Jealousy, and Hatred hoping to destroy our relationship with the Father.

To Satan we are nothing more than pawns in his war against God. If we let him defeat us our souls we'll become trophies that are collected on the mantel above the fiery pits of Hell. Evil knows it cannot win the war for the souls of mankind, so it wants to take as many souls to Hell as it possibly can.

> "Be self-controlled and alert. Your enemy the devil prowls around like a roaring lion looking for someone to devour. Resist him, standing firm in the faith, because you know that your brothers throughout the world are undergoing the same kind of sufferings" (1 Peter 5:8).

How can we help the Undercover Angels fight Satan and his forces? We can start by volunteering to be an Undercover Angel, so that God's message of love and hope will spread worldwide. There are people who will not accept the Message, but there are many who are waiting to embrace it with all they have. So remember that even the smallest act of kindness can make the biggest difference in a person's life.

The Undercover Angels accept the assignments given to them by God. They make the choice to help others. Their personal wants and desires take a back seat to the needs of others. They are heavenly instruments that have changed the lives of so many people and brought them to the path of God.

God freely gives us the choice to choose which side of the battlefield we are on. He wants us on His side. Can we make the same unselfish choices that the Undercover Angels make every day? We need to decide where we stand in our war and on which side we are on…Good or Evil.

"Today I am giving you a choice between good and evil, between life and death" (Deuteronomy 30:15).

Remember this is your war and your choice…choose wisely. Where your soul spends eternity depends on it.

The Undercover Angels have given us this special message:

The Father has sent us from above
As a sign of His Eternal Love
To guide, protect, and comfort you
During times of trouble and joyous one too
So have no fear for we are always here
A gift from God
His gift of Love
Sent to you from High Above.

Printed in the United States
67125LVS00005B/313-360

9 781424 113170